Promoting
Sustainable
Economies
in the Balkans

Promoting Sustainable Economies in the Balkans

Report of an Independent Task Force
Sponsored by the
Council on Foreign Relations

Steven Rattner, Chairman
Michael B.G. Froman, Project Director

BOK 3010-1/2

The Council on Foreign Relations, Inc., a nonprofit, nonpartisan national organization and think tank founded in 1921, is dedicated to promoting understanding of international affairs through the free and civil exchange of ideas. The Council's members are dedicated to the belief that America's peace and prosperity are firmly linked to that of the world. From this flows the Council's mission: to foster America's understanding of other nations— their peoples, cultures, histories, hopes, quarrels, and ambitions—and thus to serve our nation through study and debate, private and public.

THE COUNCIL TAKES NO INSTITUTIONAL POSITION ON POLICY ISSUES AND HAS NO AFFILIATION WITH THE U.S. GOVERNMENT. ALL STATE-MENTS OF FACT AND EXPRESSIONS OF OPINION CONTAINED IN ALL ITS PUBLICATIONS ARE THE SOLE RESPONSIBILITY OF THE AUTHOR OR AUTHORS.

The Council will sponsor an Independent Task Force when (1) an issue of current and critical importance to U.S. foreign policy arises, and (2) it seems that a group diverse in backgrounds and perspectives may, nonetheless, be able to reach a meaningful consensus on a policy through private and nonpartisan deliberations. Typically, a Task Force meets between two and five times over a brief period to ensure the relevance of its work.

Upon reaching a conclusion, a Task Force issues a report, and the Council publishes its text and posts it on the Council's website. Task Force Reports can take three forms: (1) a strong and meaningful policy consensus, with Task Force members endorsing the general policy thrust and judgments reached by the group, though not necessarily every finding and recommendation; (2) a report stating the various policy positions, each as sharply and fairly as possible; or (3) a "Chairman's Report," in which Task Force members who agree with the Chairman's Report may associate themselves with it, while those who disagree may submit dissenting statements. Upon reaching a conclusion, the Task Force may ask individuals who were not members of the Task Force to associate themselves with the Task Force Report to enhance its impact. All Task Force Reports "benchmark" their findings against current administration policy in order to make explicit areas of agreement and disagreement. The Task Force is solely responsible for its report. The Council takes no institutional position.

For further information about the Council or this Task Force, please write the Council on Foreign Relations, 58 East 68th Street, New York, NY 10021, or call the Director of Communications at (212) 434-9400. Visit our website at www.cfr.org.

CONTENTS

FOREWORD

The conflict in Kosovo, less than four years after the brutal civil war in Bosnia, was a wake-up call to the international community. The West and others had once again underestimated the powerful forces of ethnic hatred and historical grievances in the Balkans. Thousands were killed, hundreds of thousands forced to leave their homes, and the cost of rebuilding will run into the tens of billions of dollars. Although economic reconstruction alone will not be sufficient to bring long-term peace and stability to the region, rising living standards could create tangible incentives to work toward those goals and help reduce political tensions. However, there can be little hope for peace and economic progress unless NATO continues to maintain security in the region.

The international community is involved in the region and is contributing substantial financial support to the reconstruction effort. Still, the Balkan countries can only count on this support for a relatively short period of time—perhaps a few years. The question is whether these countries can achieve sustainable growth rates and sufficient income levels, or whether some will remain international welfare states. At stake is not only the future of Kosovo and the rest of the Balkans, but also the international community's capacity to manage such situations and promote economic growth and stability in regions ravaged by conflict.

Money itself is not the issue. The key to sustainable economic growth for these countries will be their capacity to attract investment, and this will require reform. To varying degrees, the process has already started. However, after four decades of socialism, a decade of inconsistent efforts, and the repeated outbreak of conflict and war, the Balkan countries have a long way to go.

The Council formed this Independent Task Force specifically to examine whether and how the Balkan countries can achieve sustainable economic growth. The Task Force gave special attention to what the countries need to do to attract investment and what the donor community and international financial institutions can do to help.

In assessing the prospects for sustainable economic growth in the region, the Task Force came to two broad conclusions. First, to create an environment likely to attract investment, it is important to deal not only with a range of macroeconomic and structural reforms, but also with political instability, corruption, organized crime, legal and regulatory reform, and the building of civil society and institutions.

Second, the Task Force found that the prospect of integration into the European Union has the potential to be the single most important factor in creating a powerful political dynamic that helps move difficult reforms forward and contains regressive nationalist and ethnic impulses. However, to have that effect, those prospects must be real and there must be real gains for real reforms.

The Task Force recognized the special challenges that Kosovo faces. It recommended that the international community be proactive and forward-leaning in interpreting its mandate so as to provide the financial and political support necessary to establish security and economic stability and growth.

With regard to Serbia, the Task Force concluded that the international community should review its policy with the goal of striking a balance between isolating Slobodan Milosevic and his supporters on the one hand, and mitigating the effect of sanctions on the Serb people and the neighboring countries, on the other.

The Task Force recommends an ambitious plan of action for all the parties seeking to promote stability and prosperity in the Balkans. The bulk of the responsibility, of course, lies with the countries in the region themselves. If the countries in the region take the necessary steps to address their problems, the international community should be there to support them. If not, there is little that money alone can do.

These countries face complex, long-term problems. Under the best of circumstances, the Balkans are likely to face economically hard times for many years to come. In forwarding this report now when Kosovo and the rest of the Balkans are no longer in the daily headlines, the Council hopes to keep the European Union and United States focused on the long-term challenge of promoting economic sustainability in the Balkans, and also on the high political and economic costs of failure to meet that challenge. Europe is undergoing a historic process of integration that promises to strengthen the foundations of peace across the continent in the 21st century. Further outbreaks of ethnic conflict in the Balkans, however, could upset that process and start a contagion of violence that will be even more costly to contain than what the international community now faces in Bosnia and Kosovo.

We were fortunate to have Steven Rattner, deputy chairman of Lazard Frères & Co., a major investment bank, chair the Task Force. He presided over this enterprise with great skill, a powerful desire to command the facts, and a deep caring about the people of the Balkans—and the need for the international community to straighten out its act on helping people left desperate by conflict. Michael Froman, a senior fellow at the Council and at the German Marshall Fund who previously served in the White House and the Treasury Department, did a superb job as project director, bringing exceptional expertise and dedication to the effort. His sense of professionalism, talent, and dedication were clear to all throughout this effort. On behalf of the Council, I thank them for their time and contributions. Finally, I would like to thank Fondation Bogette for its generous financial support of this important endeavor.

Leslie H. Gelb
President
Council on Foreign Relations
January 2000

ACKNOWLEDGMENTS

I am enormously grateful to the chairman of the Task Force, Steve Rattner, for being so generous with his time and energy throughout this project. In addition to bringing great private sector expertise to the table, Steve kept the Task Force focused on the key issues and was tremendously effective in forging consensus out of diverse perspectives.

We would also like to extend our thanks to everyone who gave so generously of their time in connection with our meetings in Washington, D.C., New York, Brussels, and throughout the Balkans. We owe a particularly great debt of gratitude to our colleagues on the Task Force who provided invaluable input based on their wide-ranging backgrounds and experience.

Haleh Nazeri and Jessica Duda provided important research and administrative assistance, and Colonel Stanley McChrystal was instrumental in organizing our fact-finding missions to Brussels and the Balkans. The writing and editing of this report was helped considerably by our consultant, Bill Primosch.

At the Council, Les Gelb, Mike Peters, and their colleagues were extremely supportive and offered excellent guidance throughout. In addition, I am personally grateful to Craig Kennedy, Steve Grand, and the German Marshall Fund for their guidance and support during this project.

Michael B.G. Froman
Project Director

EXECUTIVE SUMMARY

After two wars, thousands of deaths, hundreds of thousands of displaced persons, and billions of dollars in destruction, the importance of stability in the Balkans cannot be ignored. Historical grievances, ethnic rivalries, and the political ambition of misguided leaders have all played important roles in triggering these conflicts. But the region's many economic problems— poverty, unemployment, stagnating economies, and a pervasive lack of hope for a better future—have contributed to an environment that made such conflicts possible. Creating sustainable economic growth and increasing standards of living cannot solve the region's political and ethnic problems. But they can contribute to stability in the region and create incentives to avoid conflict. At issue is whether the economies of this region will become sustainable over time or whether they will become or remain largely dependent on foreign assistance. Drawing on a broad range of expertise in international business and investment, the Task Force has sought to provide practical recommendations that will help policymakers in and outside the region meet this challenge.

FINDINGS

- Macroeconomic conditions vary markedly within the region. All of the Balkan countries are struggling to make the transition to market economies. They have substantial work ahead to establish ongoing, stable macroeconomic environments.

- There are numerous obstacles, particularly at the microeconomic level, to attracting investment to the region. In general, privatization of publicly owned companies has proceeded badly and failed to produce a strong, competitive private sector. The banking system is weak, both financially and institutionally, and lends mainly to governments and state enterprises rather than to the private sector. Small national economies are insufficiently integrated into markets around them.

- Some of the greatest challenges to economic sustainability are noneconomic. Political instability and the potential for conflict, violence, and war are powerful disincentives for investment. Corruption is pervasive in both government and the private sector. Legal systems are weak, with inadequate laws, unpredictable legal changes, and ineffective enforcement.

- The continuing isolation of Serbia remains a major stumbling block to economic stability and development in the region. Countries in the region are paying a heavy economic price because of the loss of Serbia's market and the need to divert shipments around transportation bottlenecks on the Danube River and elsewhere in the transportation network.

- Kosovo poses special problems for economic recovery because of its need for wide-ranging reconstruction assistance and because of its unique political status. The resolution of conflicting property claims between ethnic Serbs, Albanian Kosovars, and other stakeholders represents a serious obstacle to the revitalization and reform of the economy.

- Notwithstanding many serious obstacles to private investment, the region also has important advantages that, under the right conditions, could prove attractive to investors. The Balkan countries are close to major markets, notably the European Union (EU) and Turkey. They have the prospect of integration into the EU. And they enjoy a relatively well-educated, low-cost workforce and some promising sectors for investment.

- The EU and the United States have undertaken important new initiatives under the Stability Pact to promote regional cooperation and economic sustainability. Questions remain, however, about whether, particularly in the EU's case, they go far enough.

RECOMMENDATIONS

- Macroeconomic stability needs to be achieved and maintained. At present, the record of countries in the region is mixed. A key fiscal challenge is to control government spending, including by restricting expenditures on unprofitable publicly owned enterprises and reforming the tax system to improve revenue collection. On the monetary front, the countries in the region should ensure the political independence of their central banks and adopt a clear mandate to maintain price stability. And each country needs to evaluate its own situation carefully in establishing its exchange rate regime, bearing in mind the pros and cons of options, such as the adoption of the euro, that could restrict economic policy flexibility.

- Countries should devote much greater effort to microeconomic issues, structural reform, and completing the transition to market economies. Macroeconomic stability alone is not a sufficient condition for sustainable economic development. Governments need to take actions to make changes in corporate governance and create opportunities for foreign strategic investors to bring in capital, advanced technology, and management expertise. Regulations governing the creation and operation of private-sector enterprises need to be liberalized. The financial system—in particular, the relationship between governments and banks—needs fundamental reform to create well-regulated, well-supervised market-oriented banking systems.

- Crucial noneconomic challenges, such as political stability, legal reform, institution-building, and corruption, also must be addressed. Democratic political systems need to function effectively and prevent the outbreak of ethnic conflict and violence. Governments, with the support of the donor community, need to adopt modern market-oriented laws and regulations, create reliable processes for enforcing those laws and regulations, clarify property rights (including resolution of competing claims to publicly owned property), and establish and enforce bankruptcy procedures. The international donor community needs to be more forceful in insisting that countries fight corruption and respond with appropriate technical assistance.

- The region should create more open markets. To expand regional trade and investment, countries should reduce or eliminate trade barriers, harmonize customs procedures, and work together to develop economically sensible infrastructure projects in the region.

- The EU needs to articulate more clearly and credibly a path toward European integration that is seen as a "Partnership for Prosperity." The answer is not to lower EU standards for membership but to find a way to meaningfully engage these countries throughout the long process of accession. The partnership needs to offer, in quite specific terms, intermediate steps that the countries in the region can take and that the EU would reward—in terms of closer integration—as they proceed toward membership. For the strongest reformers, this could include a progression in stages from participation in a free trade arrangement to a customs union to the common market leading eventually to membership.

- In the interim, the EU and the United States should consider expanding their unilateral trade preferences for exports from the region, including such sensitive sectors as textiles and agriculture.

- To maximize their effectiveness in the region, the United States, EU, and international financial institutions need to improve their performance in several key areas, including diplomatic engagement, aid coordination and disbursement, and support for technical assistance. The donor community should also consult more closely with the private sector in developing its economic strategy for the region.

- The international community, including the bilateral donors and international financial institutions, should use conditionality as a core principle in their assistance strategy for the region. The governing principle should be that the international community provides the greatest support to countries that make the strongest efforts and more limited support to the region's laggards.

- Decisive action needs to be taken by the international donor community to speed up the flow of emergency humanitarian aid to Kosovo to provide for basic needs and to provide sufficient resources to the U.N. Mission in Kosovo (UNMIK) to pay doctors, teachers, and other essential government employees.

- To get the economic reform process moving, the EU and United States need to support a broad interpretation of UNMIK's mandate so that it has sufficient authority to revitalize and reform Kosovo's economy. This includes giving UNMIK the capacity to resolve competing claims over enterprise assets—including those of Belgrade and Serb-owned businesses—in such a way as to permit private investment and management pending final resolution of Kosovo's political status.

- The United States and the EU should review their policy toward Serbia with the goal of assessing the balance between isolating Slobodan Milosevic and his supporters, on the one hand, and mitigating the effect of sanctions on the Serb

people and the neighboring countries, on the other. Specifically, the United States and the EU should consider whether
there is a responsible way to expand engagement, including
additional humanitarian and reconstruction aid, to alleviate
the effects of the sanctions on the Serb people and the
neighboring countries without significantly relieving pressure on Milosevic.

REPORT

INTRODUCTION

The importance of creating stability in the Balkans is critical. Marked by ethnic conflict, political turmoil, and violence, the region has been the locus of numerous wars during the past century. Two have occurred in just the past five years, first in Bosnia and then in Kosovo. Turmoil in the Balkans reverberates far beyond the immediate region. Thus, stability there is of vital importance to Europe, to the United States, and to the entire international community.

At stake is not only the future of Kosovo and the rest of the Balkans, but also the international community's capacity to manage such situations and to promote economic growth and stability in regions ravaged by conflict. At issue is whether the Balkan countries can achieve sustainable economic growth and increased standards of living or whether some will become or remain largely dependent on foreign assistance.

Although the wars in the Balkans are over, at least for now, the potential for further conflict remains and the process of building a stable peace has a distance to go. For the foreseeable future, a NATO military presence will be essential for keeping the peace in Kosovo and Bosnia and providing a sense of security to the entire region. But going beyond that to deal with the root causes of conflict in the Balkans will be more difficult. They are many and complex, rooted in historical grievances and the political ambitions of misguided leaders. Although not a central cause, economic issues have played a role in contributing to the overall context that gave rise to conflicts in the Balkans. Sustainable economic growth and increasing prosperity by themselves are not sufficient to bring long-term peace and stability to the region, but rising standards of living could help reduce political tensions and create tangible incentives to work toward those goals.

The bulk of responsibility for the success or failure of the region lies with the countries in the region themselves. The need for action is urgent. The support and attention of the international community is a wasting asset, and the countries in the region have only a few years to demonstrate real progress before the focus of the international community turns elsewhere.

Some have called for a new Marshall Plan, but the analogy is faulty. The Marshall Plan rebuilt the economic infrastructure that existed in prewar Europe. The challenge in the Balkans is to lay the foundations for a market economy where none previously existed. Moreover, money is not the issue. If the amount of international aid is calculated as a percentage of the GDP of the countries in the region, the international community has already committed far more than what was involved in reconstructing post–World War II Europe. What is critical is reform. At base, the ball is in the Balkans' court. If the Balkan countries are willing to address their challenges, the international community should be there to support them. If not, there is little that external assistance alone can do to create sustainable economic growth, increased standards of living, and stable economies over time.

Under the best of circumstances, the Balkans are likely to face economically hard times for many years to come. However, if the countries in the region, assisted by the United States, the European Union (EU), and international financial institutions, fail to do everything they can to improve those prospects, the economic situation in the Balkans could create an ongoing threat to peace and stability in Europe. Addressing the underlying problems—such as the absence of basic structures of civil society and a market economy—could make a decisive difference and avoid potentially larger costs later on. The objective of this Task Force is to make recommendations on how best to approach this challenge.

Report

THE BALKAN REGION AND ITS ECONOMIC CONDITIONS

Although at the frontier of western Europe, certain Balkan economies are in some respects similar to developing countries. They are relatively poor. They have underdeveloped infrastructure and weak legal and regulatory regimes. And they are struggling to make the transition to market economies, a challenge made more difficult by the impact of recent wars in the region.

The Task Force focused on seven countries: Albania, Bosnia, Bulgaria, Croatia, Yugoslavia (including Kosovo and Montenegro), the Former Yugoslav Republic of Macedonia, and Romania.[1] With a total population of 53 million, or 14 percent of the EU total, the Balkans are roughly the size of France or the United Kingdom, but the region has an annual GDP of only $108 billion, or about 1 percent of the EU's GDP. Per capita GDP ranges from an estimated $400 in Kosovo to approximately $4,500 in Croatia, and the region's average per capita GDP is less than 7 percent of the EU's average. The region's industrial sector is largely based on antiquated and obsolete technology. Agriculture remains an important sector in Balkan countries, accounting for 10 percent to 50 percent of GDP, compared with 5 percent in the EU.

Historically, Yugoslavia was more prosperous, more modern, and more market oriented than other socialist countries, including Poland. After 10 years of political instability and conflict, however, Yugoslavia's constituent parts have seen their economic position erode as others have pressed ahead with reforms. Similarly, as a result of political fragility, Albania, Romania, and Bulgaria have lagged behind other former socialist countries in making the transition to market economies, despite 10 years of effort and engagement by the international community. The Kosovo conflict only made the transition effort more challenging.

---

[1] We did not include Slovenia because it appears to be on a faster track to EU membership and is already stable, relatively prosperous, and more fully integrated into European markets.

The Balkans are not monolithic, and, therefore, it is difficult to generalize about the region. While all of the Balkan countries share certain challenges, including making the transition to market economies, some face far more fundamental challenges that go to the core of their viability as independent states. For places such as Albania, Bosnia, and Kosovo, an inability to establish public order and governance, the constant potential for ethnic conflict and violence, a near total lack of rule of law, and the corrosive effect of organized crime loom large on their list of concerns. Still, addressing their macroeconomic and structural challenges is also important and, in fact, can be a critical mechanism for creating an environment in which they can deal with some of these more basic concerns. The brief description of the countries that follows is intended to give a flavor of the diversity of the region and put each country's economic challenges in the context of the overall situation it faces.

Bulgaria suffered a serious economic crisis in 1997 that brought about a change in government and economic policies. A disciplined program of economic reform, combined with the adoption of a currency board, tamed Bulgaria's hyperinflation, bringing it down to about 4 percent per annum. The changes also helped generate a budget surplus of 2.8 percent of GDP in 1998. Bulgaria's economy grew at an annual rate of 3.5 percent in 1998 and continued to expand in 1999. Bulgaria is also making progress in tackling its structural issues. Although much remains to be done, privatization is proceeding, regulations on private economic activity have been liberalized, and serious and relatively successful efforts have been made to attack organized crime and corruption.

Romania presents a more mixed picture. With 23 million inhabitants, Romania is the largest market in the region and has attracted a fair amount of interest from foreign investors. However, it has had substantial difficulty achieving macroeconomic stability and adhering to its International Monetary Fund (IMF) programs. The Romanian government has had serious problems maintaining fiscal discipline, partly due to the relatively high degree of independence with which parts of Romania's government operate in its coalition-based political system. Romania continues to have an annual inflation rate of about 50 percent. Its GDP fell 7.3 percent in 1998, and a further decline is expected for 1999.

In addition to its macroeconomic difficulties, Romania has been slow to pursue microeconomic and structural reforms. Corruption remains pervasive, both in the public and the private sectors. The legal system is unreliable. Where privatization has occurred, it has been done poorly, and much remains in state hands. The banking system lends little to the private sector, transferring resources instead to the government and government-owned enterprises.

Croatia is in many respects more economically developed than other countries in the region. Geographically and culturally, it is closer to the rest of Europe. Still, it faces serious economic problems, and its political situation has stymied reform, preventing it from joining the first tier of countries eligible for EU membership. Zagreb is not an international pariah like Belgrade, but Croatia has faced a degree of isolation for the last several years as a result of the late President Franjo Tudjman's conduct in a number of areas, such as cooperation on war criminal and refugee issues.

On the economic front, Croatia faces significant fiscal pressures. Its banking system is weak, insufficiently regulated, and prone to crony lending. The Croatian economy suffers a serious arrearages problem with significant delays in payments among the government, state-owned enterprises, and the private sector. Much has been privatized, but most enterprises remain under the control of managers and workers who lack the capital and expertise to improve enterprise efficiency. Excessive regulations are impeding the creation of new businesses as are high labor costs, which include large government-mandated social charges. The reform agenda, as well as most foreign investment, has been on hold awaiting Tudjman's death and the recent elections.

Albania is the poorest country in Europe, with a per capita GDP of $810 a year. It has little industry and relies heavily on an inefficient agricultural sector. Albania's leaders, working closely with the international financial institutions and donor community, have begun to pursue an economic reform agenda, including in the areas of banking, legal, and regulatory reform. However, at present there is little effective governance outside of Tirana. The legal process, regulatory regime, and banking system barely function. The bulk of economic activity is in the unofficial sector, the country is rife with corruption, and organized crime has virtually free rein to carry out illegal activities. With all these problems, Albania is likely to remain dependent on foreign aid for years to come.

Bosnia has made significant progress on reconstruction and enjoys an artificial degree of macroeconomic stability, thanks to the currency board arrangement and massive, but likely temporary, flows of foreign assistance. GDP increased by an estimated 30 percent in 1998 and continued to grow at a good clip in 1999, but that is almost entirely due to transfer payments. Bosnia's domestic output has increased only marginally.

Notwithstanding some improvement over the past year, ethnic-nationalist rivalries continue to hamper effective governance, including in the realm of economic reform. The remnants of the former Yugoslav payments system, a mechanism through which the state monitors, controls, and executes all financial transactions, continue to stifle the development of a real banking system. The privatization process risks being hijacked by political parties eager to assert control over state assets for the exclusive use of one ethnic community or another. Multiple approvals are required to start new businesses, reinforcing pervasive corruption within government. As a result, there has been almost no foreign investment and little growth of private enterprise. The Bosnian economy remains substantially dependent on foreign aid and vulnerable to overall decline when these aid flows decrease—as they almost inevitably will.

Macedonia is mainly an agricultural economy, but it also has limited industry, including a large textile sector. However, even this sector tends to produce only low value-added outputs. The privatization of Macedonia's state-owned assets has generally not led to new corporate governance or increased investment. As does much of the rest of the region, Macedonia suffers from a weak banking system. To maintain its exchange rate, Macedonia's interest rates run as high as 17 to 25 percent. Banks buy government debt and bail out state-owned enterprises, but entrepreneurs complain that they are unable to obtain credit for projects they view as creditworthy. To compensate for its small domestic market, the Macedonian government is attempting to position itself as a hub for regional trade by negotiating a network of free trade agreements and supporting a range of cross-border infrastructure projects.

Kosovo poses special issues. At present, its economy is driven entirely by the beginnings of the $3 billion in promised aid flows and the remittances of the Kosovar diaspora. Almost nothing is being produced, as most industrial facilities cannot operate due to war damage, lack of electrical power, the absence of key personnel, or years of inadequate plant and equipment maintenance. Whatever legitimate economic activity does exist is generally limited to small-scale retail trade. On the positive side, the U.N. Mission in Kosovo (UNMIK) has taken important initial steps to establish a stable economic framework. Restrictions on the deutsche mark have been lifted, and it now serves as the de facto currency of choice for both official and private economic activity. UNMIK has also begun to create a fiscal system for Kosovo (e.g., by collecting excise and customs taxes at border crossings and by developing detailed government budgets). However, UNMIK faces serious problems in securing early disbursements from the international donor community to pay the salaries of Kosovo's public sector, including teachers and doctors.

Restarting commercial enterprises will not be easy. There is great confusion over competing Serb and Albanian property claims, which creates a cloud of uncertainty over the status of major publicly owned assets. The United Nations is struggling to reconcile the tension between the two components of U.N. Security Council Resolution 1244, which calls on the United Nations to promote greater self-rule for Kosovo, but to do so within the sovereignty of Yugoslavia and without prejudging Kosovo's ultimate status. At issue is whether the United Nations will be able to develop a coherent approach to managing this tension and at the same time pursue the reform and revitalization of Kosovo's economy.

That leaves the rest of Yugoslavia: Serbia and Montenegro. As we write, Montenegro is inching toward greater autonomy, including by recognizing the deutsche mark as acceptable currency for official uses. It is unclear whether this movement will result in independence or some continued but loose arrangement with Serbia, and whether this transition will be violent or peaceful. Clearly, though, Montenegro is looking to differentiate itself, politically and economically, from its Serb neighbor.

Serbia stands alone within the region, politically isolated and in an economic chasm. Serbia's economy had been declining since the breakup of Yugoslavia in 1991 because of economic mismanagement, Western economic sanctions, and the war in Bosnia. Now price increases are again nearing hyperinflation rates. Its reserves are depleted, and its infrastructure and key industrial facilities are severely damaged. Without Western aid, energy and consumer goods shortages are likely to impose severe hardships in urban areas throughout the winter. Figures regarding the war damage are difficult to verify, but reconstruction estimates run from $30 billion to $100 billion.

Serbia is now the proverbial hole in the Balkan doughnut. Its isolation has disrupted trade flows throughout the region, requiring its neighbors to seek alternative, more expensive routes to Europe's markets. Ultimately, it is very much in the interests of both Serbia and its neighbors that it be reintegrated into the region, but with Slobodan Milosevic still in power, there is no consensus within the international community to do so.

In sum, this is a region facing serious economic challenges. There are some steps that can be taken immediately; others will take several years to accomplish. And even if these steps are taken, we should avoid raising unreasonable expectations. The Balkans is a poor and troubled region of the world that is unlikely to become a major destination for foreign investment. Yet, as discussed below, the region enjoys certain advantages, and with the right policies and international support, it could significantly improve its economic performance and reduce its dependence on foreign assistance.

The international community's goals for the region should be to establish stability and growth on a sustainable basis. The bulk of the responsibility lies with the countries in the region themselves, but they will need the support of the United States, the EU, and the international financial institutions to succeed.

MAJOR ISSUES FACING THE REGION'S ECONOMIES

To achieve sustainable economic growth, the countries in the Balkans must attract private investment from home and abroad.[2] A number of organizations, including the World Bank, the Organization for Economic Cooperation and Development (OECD), the Stability Pact's Economic Table, and the Transatlantic Business Dialogue have done good work in analyzing major factors that influence decisions to invest. Rather than repeat the full list here, we have focused on some of the most critical issues that pose particular concern in the Balkans.

---

[2] Foreign investment is an important source not only of capital, but also technology and management expertise. That said, few countries have achieved economic sustainability without mobilizing domestic savings and investment as well, given that foreign investors are unlikely to make sizable investments in countries whose own citizens are not prepared to invest.

One general observation: There is a perception by some in the region that pursuing sound fiscal and monetary policies constitutes economic success. Clearly, sound macroeconomic policies are necessary, and a number of the countries in the region have much to do to meet that threshold, but they are not sufficient. The donor community and international financial institutions have made an effort to press the governments in the region to privatize their state-owned assets, reform their legal and regulatory regimes, strengthen their financial systems, etc. However, work toward these objectives, many of which are long-term in nature, unpopular and difficult to achieve, frequently lags as a lower priority. In some cases, this reflects a lack of commitment or outright opposition by leaders in the region to the reform agenda. In others, it reflects a lack of the necessary political or technical capacity to take on these challenges.

Corruption and Organized Crime

Potential investors cite organized crime and corruption at or near the top of their list of concerns. For the most part, the major problem is the pervasiveness of corruption, but in some parts of the region, organized crime has become so institutionalized as to pose an additional threat. Southeast Europe is certainly not unique in facing the problems of crime and corruption, but they are as pervasive and corrosive there as virtually anywhere in the world. And they not only limit economic development but also pose a potentially serious threat to the region's emergent democratic institutions. Some of the problems in this arena are endemic to transition economies; others are specific to the region.

In Albania, the weakness of the government has given rise to widespread lawlessness, with criminal organizations operating freely throughout the country. In Kosovo, there is great concern about organized crime groups taking root. The region as a whole has become a major transit route for drugs, arms, and other contraband, and it now houses criminal networks that extend well into western Europe.

Corruption is prevalent throughout the region in both the public and private sectors. In the public sector, requirements for multiple approvals, lack of transparency (particularly in the privatization process), and the lack of reliable enforcement of laws and regulations have created an environment in which corruption has flourished and deterred investment. As the region's private sector grows, corruption (e.g., in enterprises' procurement decisions) is becoming increasingly embedded in the region's business culture as well.

Weak Legal Systems

A separate but related concern is the weakness of the legal systems in the region. Problems arise not only from the inadequacy of laws but the manner in which they are (or are not) enforced. Potential investors cite three types of problems. First, some of the countries in the region have yet to adopt laws that are key to a functioning market economy, including bankruptcy laws and modern commercial codes. Second, there are serious concerns about the stability or reliability of the legal system. As one foreign investor stated, "We can deal with almost any law, as long as we can plan on the basis of it and it doesn't change every six months." Third, there are serious concerns about how well judges understand the laws they are applying, as well as concerns about delays in the execution of their judgments and the honesty and independence of the judicial process.

One of the most significant obstacles to investment in the Balkans is the lack of clarity over property rights. Throughout much of the region, there are unresolved claims based on the post–World War II expropriation of private property by socialist governments. Furthermore, there is a second level of uncertainty based on claims emerging from ethnic conflicts. In Bosnia, for example, there are competing claims to property arising out of shifts in populations caused by the war, with one ethnic community living in homes previously owned by another. In

Kosovo, as previously mentioned, a major challenge for UNMIK will be whether it can encourage economic reform and private investment given the competing property claims of Serbs, ethnic Albanians, and other stakeholders in publicly owned enterprises.

Faulty Privatization

Progress on privatization varies from one country to the next, but with few exceptions, it has not yet produced a strong competitive, market-oriented private sector. In most cases, the privatization process lacked transparency. There was favoritism toward insiders and, either through management-employee buyouts or voucher programs, the assets ended up in the hands of former state managers and workers who lacked the capital, the expertise, or the strong desire to reform the enterprises. As a result, the privatization process has tended either to encourage asset-stripping by former socialist managers or to produce state-sanctioned monopolies that continue to prevent the emergence of private sector competitors.

Weak Financial Systems

One of the most serious obstacles to mobilizing private investment, particularly from domestic sources, is the weakness of the banking system and the absence of capital markets, a legacy of 50 years of socialism. After successive banking crises, many people in the region distrust their domestic financial institutions and keep a large portion of whatever savings they have "under the mattress." The public's lack of confidence in the domestic banking system reflects, in part, the absence of a professional, apolitical regulatory and supervisory regime and the lack of a deposit insurance scheme in most of these countries. Foreign banks have either not been permitted or have been reluctant to fill the void, and only a small number operate in the region.

Domestic banks in the region are not substantial lenders to the private sector. Instead, they tend to purchase government debt and lend to those state-owned or state-controlled enterprises to which they are captive. This is partly a legacy of government planning in which banks' primary role was to finance government budget deficits and provide working capital to state-owned or, in the case of Yugoslavia, socially owned, enterprises. But the domestic banks' failure to lend to the private sector also reflects a lack of credit culture in the region. Banks lack the technical expertise to assess the creditworthiness of potential borrowers and make lending decisions on commercial grounds. The result is that the private sector cannot obtain the capital that it believes it could use productively to start and expand businesses.

Small, Poor Markets

With the exception of Romania, individual countries in the region are generally too small to attract large-scale foreign investment to serve their relatively poor, domestic markets. Of course, as a number of other small countries (e.g., Switzerland and Singapore) demonstrate, the disadvantage of having a small domestic market can be overcome by integration into larger markets. If the countries in the region create open, reformed economies, they might well be attractive to investors as a platform for production for all of southeast Europe, the European Union, and other export markets.

The region's relationship with the EU is complicated and will be discussed in further detail below. According to the EU, more than 80 percent of the region's exports now enter the EU duty free and even where quantitative restraints are in effect, exports from this region have tended to remain below the designated quota levels. The perspective of the region, though, is that real barriers to the EU market remain. There are likely a number of indigenous factors, such as inadequate infrastructure and a lack of competitive production capacity, that may be preventing Balkan region exporters from fully accessing the EU. However, it is also likely that the perception of remaining barriers to the EU market is discouraging investment and development of production capacity in the region.

Within the Balkans, there are still serious barriers to trade, including tariffs, nontariff barriers, inefficient and corrupt customs administrations, and transportation bottlenecks. Moreover, as a general matter, regional cooperation on economic and other issues of common concern does not come naturally to the Balkans today.

The Problem of Serbia and Milosevic

Serbia under Milosevic's leadership remains a major stumbling block to long-term stability and prosperity in the Balkans. Serbia is at the crossroads of the region, a key nexus of road, rail, and river transportation in the region. It has also been an important industrial base and market for the region, particularly the former Yugoslav republics. For the time being, Balkan countries have no alternative but to seek other transportation routes and to proceed in developing regional cooperation without Serbia. Its continued isolation, however, not only prevents a return to economic normalcy but also serves as a potential ongoing source of political instability and conflict in the region.

Real and Perceived Risks

The centrality of Serbia points to another important issue: real versus perceived risks. The above list, which is by no means exhaustive, illustrates many real risks that investors in the Balkans face. That said, even the most stable, safe, and reform-minded country in the region (Bulgaria) is having difficulty attracting investment because of the general perception that the Balkans is an unstable and potentially violent part of the world. This puts a premium on the international community doing what can be done to highlight the diversity of the countries in the region and to help the private sector in distinguishing between the more and less risky parts of the region. It also underscores the importance of addressing the larger issues (i.e., the promotion of a democratic Yugoslavia) affecting political stability and security in the region.

ECONOMIC ADVANTAGES

Notwithstanding the above-mentioned problems, the region enjoys certain attributes that potentially can contribute to growth and development.

Proximity to Major Markets
While the markets in the Balkans are small and underdeveloped, they are close to major markets, including the European Union with its 375 million high per capita income consumers and Turkey with its 63 million consumers.

Prospect of Integration with the European Union
Looking to the future, the prospects for sustainable economic growth in the Balkans are greatly enhanced by the possibility of their eventual integration, in some form or another, into the European Union. For some countries (e.g., Romania and Bulgaria), EU membership could come relatively quickly—in a decade or so. For others, it could take much longer. And for some, membership might never be appropriate. But in the meantime, the prospects for improving market access and closer integration could lead the countries in the region to pursue a broad array of reforms designed to bring themselves closer to Europe's standards, rules, and business practices. These changes, in turn, could make an important contribution to enhancing the investment environment in the region.

Relatively Well-Educated and Inexpensive Workforce
Despite the low levels of economic performance, the educational and literacy levels in the Balkans are relatively high compared with other countries at similar income levels. Several, such as Bulgaria, Romania, and Croatia, have large numbers

of technically skilled workers, including in software development and engineering design, who could be valuable assets to their countries if they could be effectively employed at home. Unfortunately, a significant brain drain throughout the region has siphoned off many of the most talented individuals to EU countries, Canada, and the United States. If the economic environment improves, some might return, bringing with them newly acquired business skills and possibly even investment capital.

Promising Sectors

Industrial enterprises in most of the region have deteriorated with the lack of investment in recent years. Much of their equipment is old and based on outdated technology. Still, there may be some traditional sectors, including mineral products, textiles, shoes, agro-processing, and furniture, in which enterprises in the region could serve the domestic markets competitively and that could be an important source of export earnings. Moreover, there is a surplus of electricity production capacity in the region that, with the further development in regional energy interconnection infrastructure, could also produce export earnings. Tourism remains a potentially lucrative industry as well for some countries, especially Croatia. But perhaps even more importantly, as the nascent software industries in Romania and Bulgaria illustrate, there could well be new sectors, including some in higher value-added sectors, in which greenfield investments could be competitive.

REVIEW OF U.S. AND EU POLICIES

As Serb forces withdrew from Kosovo, the international donor community swung into action. Armed with the lessons of Bosnia, positive and negative, they set out to mobilize resources and organize a reconstruction initiative. In some respects, the initial results have been impressive. But, while donor conferences have produced more than $3 billion in pledges, and more than 200 aid organizations have set up shop in Kosovo, there are serious questions about the actual pace at which reconstruction funds are being disbursed on the ground and whether Kosovars will have what they need to survive the winter.

In addition to the Kosovo reconstruction effort, the EU initiated and the United States supported the launching of the Stability Pact to bring the countries in the region together to deal with political, security, and economic issues, and to integrate them into the Euro-Atlantic community. It was designed to create simultaneously a sense of regional identity and European identity for the countries of southeast Europe. To enhance cooperation and coordination, the Stability Pact established several forums (i.e., "Tables") at which southeast European countries and donors can meet to discuss regional issues, including trade and investment, and establish a plan of action.

Under the rubric of the Stability Pact, the EU and United States have announced a variety of new aid and trade initiatives to promote recovery and economic development in the Balkans. The EU will be the largest source of foreign assistance to the Balkans. In 2000–06, the EU is planning to extend aid amounting to 5.5 billion euros to Albania and the former Yugoslav republics and Kosovo, and 6.0 billion euros to Romania and Bulgaria.[3]

The United States has pledged to provide $157 million for aid to Kosovo in 2000 and announced other initiatives to promote development throughout the Balkans. The U.S. Overseas Private Investment Corporation (OPIC) will create one or more private sector investment funds that will mobilize up to $150 million in financing. OPIC will also provide a $200 million credit line for commercial ventures with significant U.S. participation. Other new assistance includes $34 million to help the European Bank for Reconstruction and Development (EBRD) to develop a $130-million small and medium-size

---

[3]The euro/dollar exchange rate during 1999 fluctuated in the range of $1.01 to $1.17 = euro 1.00.

enterprise (SME) lending facility and $16 million in technical assistance on legal and regulatory reforms.

New EU and U.S. initiatives will complement and support large ongoing programs of the IMF, World Bank, and the EBRD in the region. The IMF has in place multiyear programs totaling about $2.0 billion for Albania, Bosnia, Bulgaria, Croatia, Macedonia, and Romania. World Bank programs for the six countries amount to $4.2 billion. In addition to large infrastructure projects, the World Bank is financing activities in the fields of health, community development, agricultural and forestry development, enterprise privatization, land registration, pensions, and SME development. The EBRD is focusing on supporting private sector investment and, as of June 30, 1999, had committed $2.5 billion to 107 projects in the region. All three institutions are also providing substantial technical assistance to help governments design and implement market-oriented economic reforms.

The EU has also agreed to launch membership negotiations with Bulgaria and Romania, provided certain conditions are met (e.g., Bulgaria dealing with its Chernobyl-type reactor), and—in principle—to negotiate Stabilization and Association Agreements (SAAs) with Albania and the former Yugoslav republics. The SAAs are aimed at encouraging regional integration and laying groundwork for future EU membership. The agreements would include an expansion of existing trade preferences. They would also increase assistance for democratization and institution-building, provide new opportunities for cooperation with the EU in law enforcement, and develop channels for eventual political dialogue, including at the regional level.

To date, the EU has approved the start of SAA negotiations only with Macedonia. A recent EU report on Albania cited shortcomings in the country's performance in several areas (e.g., the general weakness of the economy and ineffective governance) and left open the question whether SAA negotiations with that country would begin any time soon. Similarly, the EU has conditioned the negotiation of SAAs with Bosnia and Croatia on the settlement of issues relating to the treatment of national minorities and on the mutual recognition of each other's borders. Since these issues remain unresolved, no timetable has been set for the start of those negotiations. Yugoslavia is also potentially eligible for an SAA but no action appears possible while Milosevic is in power.

The EU is encouraging Balkan countries to pursue economic integration among themselves even as they seek integration with the EU. Although regional economic integration is not strictly a precondition for European integration, the EU has emphasized the importance of steps, such as a regional free trade arrangement, that demonstrate the readiness of the Balkan countries to participate in the EU's more intensive program of integration. While increasing regional interaction could potentially have positive economic effects, the EU proposal has been greeted with some concern in the region as an effort by the EU either to reconstitute the former Yugoslavia or to create an obstacle to meaningful European integration.

Although the United States is a much less important market for the Balkans than Europe, the United States is also taking additional steps to help promote increased trade with the region.[4] At the Sarajevo Summit in July 1999, President Clinton announced his intention to propose additional trade preferences for all the southeast European countries participating in the Stability Pact. Since then, the U.S. administration has introduced legislation that, if enacted, would permit duty-free entry to all exports from the region except for textile and apparel products. The duty-free entry would also apply to agricultural products, although imports subject to quotas will not be eligible for duty-free entry beyond the quota amount.

Despite strong European and American pledges of assistance and rhetoric in support of integration, there remains a certain amount of skepticism in the region, particularly with regard to the EU's intentions and capacity to deliver on closer integration.

---

[4]The region sells only 4 percent of its exports to the United States, with more than 80 percent going to Europe.

Well-founded or not, these perceptions are shaping the views of many people in the Balkans and influencing their willingness to support the types of efforts that are necessary to promote stability and economic recovery in the region. These concerns must be taken seriously.

ACTION PLAN

RECOMMENDATIONS

Below are a series of recommendations for actions to be taken by the governments in the region and by the international community. Some can be accomplished immediately. Others will take substantial time to complete. But even for the longer-term steps, urgent action is needed. The international community's attention is now focused on the Balkans, but this will not last. There is a relatively short period of time—a few years, perhaps—during which the countries in the region can count on substantial official financial support. A great deal needs to get done to reconstruct the countries in the region, to complete the transformation to market economies, and to create an environment that will attract the private investment needed to create sustainable economic growth. The obstacles are great but the following program would enhance the prospects of success.

Recommendation 1. Macroeconomic Stability
The countries in the region should achieve and maintain macro-economic stability. Bulgaria has made the greatest progress. However, all of the countries in the region face varying degrees of challenges on this front, from Romania, which is still struggling with double-digit inflation, to Bosnia, whose economy is supported by massive but temporary foreign assistance flows, to Macedonia, which maintains a stable currency but only through prohibitively high interest rates. Key fiscal challenges are to control government spending, including such measures as restricting expenditures on unprofitable publicly owned enterprises, and reforming the tax system to improve revenue collection. On the monetary front, the countries in the region

should ensure the political independence of their central banks and adopt a clear mandate to maintain price stability.

With regard to exchange rate policy, some governments in the region have currency boards (Bosnia, Bulgaria), others have liberalized the use of the deutsche mark (Kosovo, Montenegro), and others have linked their currencies with varying degrees of rigidity to the deutsche mark (Croatia, Macedonia). In addition, there is an ongoing debate, inside and outside the region, about whether or when some of the countries should eventually adopt the euro as their official currency, which could further facilitate integration with the European Union.

Each country needs to carefully evaluate its own situation in establishing its exchange rate regime. Currency boards, fixed rates, and euroization could help contribute to macroeconomic stability in some countries, but such policies also affect export competitiveness and require a degree of macroeconomic discipline that is difficult to sustain over time for countries engaged in a major reconstruction and transition effort.

While countries should keep their options open, including by pursuing the structural reforms (e.g., financial sector strengthening) that would be necessary to euroize their economies, some may choose to maintain a more flexible approach to exchange rates. The European Union's (EU) Exchange Rate Mechanism (ERM) offers some of the advantages of a fixed rate system but also provides flexibility in the event that economic conditions require currency adjustments. The ERM also has the advantage of being an EU instrument and thus a logical interim step toward eventual participation in the euro zone.

Whichever exchange rate policies are adopted, they must be backed by strong economic reform measures if they are to be credible and sustainable sources of macroeconomic stability over time.

Recommendation 2. Structural Reforms and Privatization
The countries in the region should devote much greater energy to microeconomic issues, structural reform, and completing the

transition to market economies. Macroeconomic stability is a necessary but not a sufficient condition for sustainable economic growth. If private investment, domestic and foreign, is to become a major source for financing growth and development, the countries in the region need to focus substantially greater attention on privatizing and restructuring state and socially owned assets; liberalizing regulations governing private sector activity and labor markets; and developing a well-regulated, well-supervised, commercially based financial sector.

Where privatization has occurred, it has tended to be done poorly, with most of the assets handed over to the existing managers and workers who have neither the money nor the market-oriented management experience necessary to reform the enterprises. The governments in the region, drawing on the experience of other transition economies and with the support of the international community, need to develop mechanisms and incentives to encourage changes in corporate governance and to create opportunities for foreign strategic investors who can bring capital, technology, and expertise to the region.

Investors in the region face a maze of regulations, licenses, and bureaucratic processes that inevitably create the potential for corruption. Moreover, they can be used too easily by officials to protect politically influential state-owned enterprises against competition. The governments in the region need to sharply reduce and substantially simplify regulations governing the establishment and operation of private sector enterprises. The objectives of the regulatory framework, such as protecting consumers, investors, or the environment, should be transparent and applied in a consistent and reliable manner.

One area of specific concern is labor market regulation. When it is difficult or costly to fire a worker, that is a significant disincentive to hire new workers. To facilitate the restructuring of privatized enterprises and the creation of new private sector jobs, the governments in the region should take steps to liberalize labor market regulation, including the rules regarding hiring, firing, and compensating workers. Of course, this is an area of significant divergence between the United States and continental Europe. Still, there is substantial room for liberalization before the Balkan countries reach even the EU level of labor market regulation.

In all of the countries in the region, the primary source of finance is bank lending. However, the banking systems, with few exceptions, are weak, undercapitalized, and poorly supervised. Moreover, in many of the countries, the government and its favored companies (often current or former publicly owned enterprises) use the bulk of available financing and crowd out new private businesses.

Several steps are necessary to create a banking system that can support a modern, market-based economy effectively. First, the public sector must reduce its budget deficits and the consequent demand on domestic savings. Second, governments need to give priority to strengthening their financial systems. This includes establishing the independence of their central banks, creating independent supervisory agencies with the authority to close failed banks, and introducing internationally accepted accounting standards. Third, governments should not direct the extension of credit. Instead, bankers should be trained to make loans on commercial grounds, and supervisory agencies should ensure that loans are made on such grounds to all borrowers, regardless of ownership. In all these reforms, the countries should draw on the extensive technical assistance available from the international community. In addition, microlending and other programs designed to support the development of small and medium-size enterprises may be useful in compensating for some of the weaknesses in the existing banking systems and in contributing in general to the development of a more robust civil society.

Recommendation 3. Legal Reforms and Institution-Building
Economic issues are but one aspect of an attractive investment climate. Of at least equal importance are political stability,

a modern legal framework and independent judiciary, well-functioning public institutions, civil society, and an effective effort to reduce corruption. These are difficult challenges because they are complex to deal with and long-term in nature. However, if they are not dealt with, there will be severe limits to what the countries in the region can expect in terms of attracting investment, as well as increasing economic growth, employment, and living standards. In the end, despite other painful economic adjustments, countries that avoid these difficult challenges are likely to remain mired in the very economic problems that have been the sources of political tension and instability in the past.

Political stability: This is a threshold issue. As long as ethnic tensions run high, public institutions and civil society divide themselves along ethnic loyalties, and the potential remains for armed conflict, the whole region will be seen as a high-risk area for investment. If the region is to attract any substantial investment, the countries in the region must work to develop democratic political systems and civil societies that can function effectively and prevent the outbreak of ethnic conflict and violence. Programs to strengthen civil society should range broadly to include the press, indigenous nongovernmental organizations, and small and medium-size commercial enterprises.

Legal reform: A number of institutions—the Stability Pact, the Transatlantic Business Dialogue, the World Bank, and the Organization for Economic Cooperation and Development (OECD), to name a few—have produced good checklists of reforms needed to improve the legal environment for investment. These include adopting modern market-oriented laws and regulations, creating reliable processes for enforcing those laws and regulations, clarifying property rights (including through the resolution of competing claims to publicly owned property), and establishing and enforcing bankruptcy procedures.

But the economic components of legal reform are part of a much larger challenge of establishing more generally the rule of law in societies in which its practice is lacking. True legal reform requires not just an understanding of private property and contracts, but a readiness to accept the equality of all persons before the law. It requires a judiciary that is not only knowledgeable about the functioning of a market system, but can act with impartiality and independence even in the face of strong political pressures. And all of this requires a political consensus of support that takes time to nurture.

The legal reforms needed in the region involve difficult, long-term challenges, but steps can be taken now to start building technical capacity and changing attitudes. The international community should explore areas where it can increase its assistance, including formal education and training, and exposure to legal systems, local government, and political activities. In designing its programs, the international community should make every effort to secure buy-in from the local communities, leverage indigenous resources (e.g., judges associations), and invest in worthwhile, but long-term projects (e.g., judicial training initiatives).

Corruption: The international donor community has expressed deep concerns about the corrosive effects of corruption in the region. It can take at least two steps immediately to help. First, the OECD Convention on Combating Bribery of Foreign Public Officials in International Business Transactions, concluded on December 17, 1997, committed all signatories to enact legislation prohibiting their nationals from engaging in such activity. In signing the convention, all signatories agreed to take steps to disallow the tax deductibility of bribes to foreign officials. Despite these commitments, several EU members (France, Italy, the Netherlands, Ireland, Portugal, and Luxembourg) have yet to make the necessary legislative changes to outlaw the bribery of foreign public officials, and in Luxembourg bribes remain tax deductible. EU members that have not already passed the enabling legislation, or have not yet excluded bribes as a tax deduction, should act promptly to do so.

Second, the international community should make corruption a threshold issue for international support, explicitly conditioning its assistance on concrete efforts to address this problem. No country has a perfect record on corruption, and it is not in the international community's interest to withhold its support for an unreasonable objective. Nonetheless, the international community can and should use its leverage to get countries in the region to take meaningful steps to deal with any serious corruption problems they face. For example, the World Bank offers countries assistance in assessing the pervasiveness of corruption and in developing an effective response. No Balkan country, however, has requested the bank's assistance. Donor governments should consider requiring countries with serious corruption problems to request a World Bank corruption audit or similar exercise as a condition of World Bank lending or bilateral donor assistance. Moreover, implementation of the series of reforms proposed by the Stability Pact Anti-Corruption Initiative, notably in the areas of customs administration, law enforcement, and the judiciary, should be started and technical assistance, as needed, should be provided.

At the Istanbul Summit in November 1999, the Stability Pact countries took a potentially useful step in all three of the aforementioned areas by endorsing a Southeast European Investment Compact. Under the compact, countries in the region agreed to improve their legal and regulatory frameworks, including those aimed at preventing corruption. The EU and the United States, in turn, pledged to make greater efforts to encourage foreign investment in those countries that are making progress in improving the investment climate. The OECD Secretariat is providing technical expertise to help countries identify key investment issues and develop a strategy for addressing them. The challenge now is to ensure that the compact actually produces reforms that affect the decisions of investors.

Recommendation 4. Economic Integration

Given the small size of most of the economies in the region, open markets will be essential in fostering innovation, competitiveness, and productivity gains. Economic growth and development in the Balkan countries will depend crucially on exports. Exports, in turn, can be fostered by trade liberalization, infrastructure development, and more intensive regional cooperation on a range of economic issues.

The opportunity for meaningful integration into the EU, discussed in greater detail in the next recommendation, could be the single most important factor in spurring on the reform necessary to achieve sustainable economic growth. While potentially helpful to economic development, neither regional cooperation nor regional integration can substitute for EU integration.

That said, regional cooperation is an area in which the countries in the region can take action now to help themselves. There is currently very little economic interaction among the countries in the region even though significant gains could be achieved by expanding trade. The reduction or elimination of trade barriers, the harmonization of customs procedures, and the development of regional infrastructure would reduce costs, expand consumer choice, and stimulate private sector development. In addition to the economic benefits, the elimination of tariffs and the harmonization of customs procedures could remove one of the most important sources of corruption in the region.

Development of regional infrastructure, including roads, railroads, telecommunications networks, electricity grids, pipelines, and bridges, would facilitate trade, improve the profitability of investments by increasing economies of scale and reducing overhead costs, and foster other interaction among the countries in the region. Once Milosevic leaves power and more normal relations with Belgrade are restored, some of the current needs for infrastructure may change, but the basic objective will not.

Much good work on infrastructure planning has already been done by EU ministers of transportation, the European Investment Bank, the Southeast Europe Cooperation Initiative, and governments in the region. At the Istanbul Summit, the Stability Pact leaders reached agreement on the process by which proposed projects should be reviewed, vetted, and approved. The international community should use that process to develop an integrated view of the region's infrastructure needs and a hard-edged assessment based on strict economic criteria, which can then provide a basis for obtaining financing.

Given the long lead time associated with infrastructure projects, governments in the region and the international community need to move ahead expeditiously to agree on priorities and pursue those infrastructure projects that are of highest priority from a regional perspective. In that regard, the ongoing dispute between Romania and Bulgaria over where to locate a second bridge over the Danube is a dramatic example of regional governments' failure to come to a common position on a potentially important project.

Care must be taken that regional infrastructure projects not be pursued on the basis of narrow national criteria or political considerations. The international community should insist on applying strict discipline in this process, based on the projects' expected rates of return, so that scarce official financial resources are not squandered on uneconomic projects.

Even with the benefit of strict discipline, careful planning, and official financing, the governments in the region face formidable obstacles in gaining access to private debt and equity markets to cofinance commercially viable infrastructure projects, especially those that cross one or more borders. As part of this effort, the donor community and international financial institutions should consider using tools at their disposal, including credit and investment enhancements, to mobilize private sources of capital for commercially viable regional infrastructure projects.

Recommendation 5. EU Integration through a Partnership for Prosperity

The EU's policies toward the Balkans and specifically the issue of future EU membership for the countries in the region, are likely to remain a source of sensitivity in U.S.-EU relations. Obviously, the United States neither can nor should attempt to dictate EU policies, particularly with regard to the integration of Balkan countries into European institutions. But given the potential for instability in the region to spill over into conflict requiring U.S. military intervention, the United States has a legitimate interest in EU decisions affecting the stability of the region. Thus, the Balkans need to remain near the top of the agenda of the transatlantic dialogue.[5]

As noted above, the EU has taken two important new initiatives related to the integration of this region into Europe. One is a pledge to start membership negotiations for Bulgaria and Romania in 2000. The other involves a proposal to create a new set of contractual arrangements—Stabilization and Association Agreements (SAAs)—for Albania and the former republics of Yugoslavia that could lay the foundation for eventual EU membership. By any measure, these initiatives, combined with the EU's pledges of assistance for the region, represent a significant step up in the EU's commitment to the Balkans.

It is our view that the European Union needs to do more. To the degree that the EU is seriously holding out the possibility of membership to all of the countries in the region, it has not effectively overcome skepticism in the region. The EU needs to articulate more clearly and credibly a path toward European integration that is seen as a genuine "Partnership for Prosperity." What is missing from the EU's current approach is a degree of specificity about the path each of the countries in the region faces and what each can expect along the way.

Making real the prospects of European integration could have a powerful impact on the political dynamic of reform in

---

[5]In that regard, the EU's efforts to reform its own structure and decision-making process in order to accommodate the accession of new member states are of critical importance—to the EU and the United States—and should be pursued expeditiously.

the region. Just as potential membership in the EU for Poland, Hungary, and the Czech Republic created a dynamic in which every policy decision was judged as to whether it brought that country closer or farther away from European integration, so too could the prospects of a European identity spur reform in the Balkans. And perhaps, just as importantly, the vision of a European future could create a powerful constraint on the capacity of nationalist or regressive forces to hijack Balkan politics.

In order for the prospects of finding a home in Europe to have the desired effects on political and economic reform, those prospects cannot be seen—as they unfortunately are now—as too remote or speculative. The key challenge for the EU is to make the path toward integration meaningful and credible without lowering its standards for membership. Indeed, it is those high standards that will drive the reforms necessary to promote political stability and economic sustainability. However, meeting these standards will take considerable time, and countries in the region are likely to advance toward membership at markedly different paces. Competition among the countries as to who will meet the standards first can be a healthy spur to reform in the region.

That is the rationale behind the proposed Partnership for Prosperity, which is intended to build upon what the EU has already announced to emphasize the EU's long-term engagement in the region and strong commitment to support its integration into the European mainstream. To be credible, the partnership needs to offer, in quite specific terms, interim and intermediate steps that the countries in the region can take and that the EU would reward—in terms of closer integration—in return.[6] Over time, the partnership could offer the strongest

---

[6] On the security front, the United States developed the concept of NATO enlargement, the Partnership for Peace, and the Russia-NATO dialogue to reflect the appropriate level of integration for different categories of countries. Recognizing that there are significant differences between joining NATO and joining the EU, the Partnership for Prosperity is nonetheless intended to be the EU analog. Some have called for "virtual membership" or associate membership. Others have talked about concentric circles or variable geography. The objective is the same: to generate meaningful ways, short of full membership in the EU, of strengthening integration and rewarding reform.

reformers in the region participation not only in a free trade arrangement, but in a customs union and a common market on the way to eventual membership. The challenge is to ensure a sufficient level of engagement—and incentives—as countries continue on the long path leading to membership. Otherwise there is a risk that countries, in the absence of seeing concrete benefits in the interim, will feel overwhelmed by the demands and lose the necessary political support for reform.

For example, given that EU membership is a long way off for Albania and the former Yugoslav republics (other than Slovenia), the EU might encourage these countries to meet the conditions for membership in the European Economic Area (EEA)—perhaps expanded to cover agricultural products as well. Doing so would strengthen ties not only between the Balkans and the EU but also among the Balkan countries themselves. Indeed, for some countries (e.g., Croatia and Bosnia), it may be politically easier to break down trade barriers between each other as part of the process of integrating with other European institutions rather than through the regional free trade negotiations the EU is currently encouraging.

As an immediate step, the EU should consider expanding its unilateral trade preferences for exports from the region. The United States should do the same, particularly with regard to textiles and apparel. Given the trade patterns, the impact on sensitive sectors will be greater in the EU than in the United States but, because of the size of the Balkan economies, that impact is likely to be marginal.

Recommendation 6. Improving the Effectiveness of Engagement in the Balkans
The international community should take steps to maximize its effectiveness in the region. While most of the responsibility for creating sustainable economies lies within the Balkan countries themselves, effective support from the international community will be critical for helping them achieve that goal. Of particular importance, the United States, the EU, and international

financial institutions should improve their performance in aid coordination and disbursement, technical assistance, and the use of conditionality.

One of the lessons of Bosnia is that whatever reforms did occur were possible only because of the constant attention and pressure of the high-level engagement of political leaders, diplomats, and economic officials. To prevent a loss of focus and an onset of complacency in the region, the United States, the EU, and international financial institutions need to resist "donor fatigue" and be prepared to devote that sort of commitment and level of economic-diplomatic resources to keep recovery and reform on track.

The international donor community has taken steps to improve its coordination, including through the creation of a joint EU-World Bank office in Brussels. Still, there continues to be confusion—in the region, in the business community, and in the donor governments—about how the several coordinating bodies (e.g., the Stability Pact, the Southeast European Cooperation Initiative, the High-Level Steering Group, and the EU-World Bank donor process) relate and how relative priorities are established for the initiatives being developed in different groups.

In Brussels and Washington, the overlapping responsibilities of numerous officials involved in Balkan recovery and reconstruction have blurred lines of authority and raised doubts about whether there is effective overall direction on Balkan policy at the highest political levels. Streamlining is needed both at the international level and within U.S. and EU bureaucracies so that there is clear leadership on overall Balkans policy and efficient mechanisms to carry out reconstruction and recovery activities in the region.

In addition, the donor community should consult closely with the private sector in developing its economic strategy for the region. A private sector group is being created to advise governments on implementing the Stability Pact's Investment

Compact. A similar group has been established by the Transatlantic Business Dialogue. The Southeast European Cooperation Initiative also has a private sector advisory group. No matter which forum proves most productive, the donor community needs to institutionalize a meaningful mechanism to bring the public and private sectors together, particularly with regard to what needs to be done to create the conditions for investment in the region.

Donors and international financial institutions need to strengthen their efforts to coordinate aid and accelerate the disbursement of assistance, particularly humanitarian aid. Delays are not only slowing reconstruction but also undercutting Western political credibility and demoralizing those in the region seeking to press ahead with reform and revitalization.

There is a great need for technical assistance, particularly with regard to the difficult challenges of institution- and capacity-building. Massive training programs are needed to produce the judges, lawyers, bankers, businesspeople, regulators, and public servants necessary to manage the transition to a market economy and effectively integrate these countries into the European Union. While there are programs in these areas, much more must be done to create the human capital necessary to carry out this project. In the past, there have been problems with donors spending aid resources on technical assistance that countries in the region were not interested in receiving and, therefore, did not use well. For technical assistance to have maximum impact, international financial institutions and countries in the region need to agree on overall objectives and strategies, and donors need to coordinate implementation to avoid duplicating efforts.

Conditionality is an essential tool for promoting change and making assistance effective. If there is one lesson to be drawn from the donor experience in Bosnia, it is that the probability of success for the foreign assistance efforts diminishes if the international community cares more about success than do people in the region. The international community, including the bilateral donors and international financial institutions, should use conditionality as a core principle in its assistance strategy for the region. Governments in the region need to understand that continued international support for reconstruction and recovery will depend on their progress in implementing key reforms, and that success brings additional rewards.

At the same time, conditions must be realistic, well-targeted, and supportive of those willing and able to implement reforms. They should take into account the political and technical capacity for change, which will differ from one country to the next. This puts a premium on donors coordinating their assistance policies and establishing reform priorities. Every aid agency cannot attach separate and distinct conditions at will, and there may be some types of assistance, such as food aid, humanitarian assistance, and some training, that should be provided without reform-linked conditionality.

There will, of course, be circumstances in which the international community will be reluctant to withhold assistance to countries that are performing poorly. But there should be a presumption that conditionality would be applied whenever feasible, as consistently as practicable, and to the greatest extent possible. The basic principle should be that the international community provides the greatest support to those countries that make the strongest efforts and more limited support to the region's laggards.

Recommendation 7. Need for Decisive Action on Emergency Aid and Reform in Kosovo
Decisive action needs to be taken to speed up the flow of emergency humanitarian aid to Kosovo. There are real concerns about the ability of many Kosovars to make it through the winter because of a lack of heat, electricity, and building materials to repair the more than 50 percent of housing damaged during the war. If the EU and United States fail to meet these basic needs, both political and economic recovery in Kosovo will suffer a serious blow that could have long-term consequences.

Nothing is likely to be accomplished in terms of political or economic stability without a strong commitment to an ongoing NATO-led presence.

In addition, there is a vital need for donors to provide the U.N. Mission in Kosovo (UNMIK) with the financial resources it needs to pay teachers, doctors, and other essential government personnel during this critical startup phase of recovery. Donors need to cut through the red tape and ensure that the Kosovo government authorities have adequate funding to provide essential services.

Over the longer term, economic reform and revitalization will be central to creating a stable environment and giving hope for the future in Kosovo. To get this process moving, the EU and United States need to support a broad interpretation of the UNMIK mandate so that it has sufficient authority to implement key reforms and take on the difficult task of settling property claims. In Kosovo, the international community faces the unique challenge of developing an economic strategy that straddles the gap between the two parts of U.N. Security Council Resolution 1244: to increase Kosovo's capacity for self-rule without compromising Belgrade's sovereignty over Kosovo or prejudging Kosovo's final status. UNMIK could interpret its mandate as follows: return Kosovo's economy to its pre-war status (by reconstructing the destroyed houses), return it to its pre-1989 status (when "the decade of silent destruction" began), or put it on the path toward market reform and sustainability (including by privatizing publicly owned assets).

It is in the interest of the international community that, regardless of its final status, Kosovo develop a sustainable economy. Therefore, the international community should work to build support within the U.N. system for UNMIK to pursue a strategy designed to achieve the broadest mandate: to reform Kosovo's economy. One specific step UNMIK could take to facilitate reform is to use its authority in Kosovo to restructure, privatize, and—to the degree it makes economic sense—revitalize state-owned industrial assets. Competing claims over enterprise assets—including those of Belgrade and Serb-owned businesses—will have to be managed in such a way as to permit private investment and management pending final resolution of Kosovo's political status. The international community should support UNMIK in resolving these issues in a proactive and pragmatic manner.

Recommendation 8. Review of Policy toward Serbia
The international community should review its policy toward Serbia with the goal of striking a pragmatic balance between isolating Slobodan Milosevic and his supporters, on one hand, and mitigating the effect of sanctions on the Serb people and the neighboring countries, on the other hand. As long as Milosevic is in power, Serbia remains a threat to stability and democracy in the region. The EU and United States, therefore, must continue to stay focused on efforts to hasten his departure. Yet it is also clear that Serbia's continued isolation and exclusion from regional development programs are seriously impeding efforts to promote regional recovery and integration and are raising costly obstacles to the expansion of trade and investment in the Balkans. The policy goals are in conflict, and the current approach should be reassessed.

Specifically, the United States and EU should consider whether expanded engagement with Serbia, including additional humanitarian and reconstruction aid, would on balance serve Western interests in the Balkans. There may be elements of the current sanctions regime that do little to weaken Milosevic's hold on power but have a disproportionately adverse impact on the Serb people or the neighboring countries. (By one theory, the current sanctions regime helps Milosevic and his supporters maintain power, because they benefit from the smuggling operations.)

For example, would the political benefits to Milosevic of rebuilding the bridges and clearing the Danube River of debris outweigh the economic costs to the region of allowing these and other transportation bottlenecks to continue? Is there more that can be done to lay the groundwork for constructive relations with the Serb people (e.g., by expanding contacts and specifying the type and scope of assistance that could be made available in the post-Milosevic era)? Is it possible to tighten sanctions on Milosevic and his close supporters (e.g., by expanding the visa ban) in ways that offset a modification of other sanctions?

Bearing in mind the goals of not only removing Milosevic from power but also building a politically stable and economically sustainable region over time, these are the kinds of questions that should be considered in deciding whether to continue or modify the current policy. However, a more thorough policy review would be needed before any changes in policy should be made.

DISSENTING VIEW

While not disagreeing with all of the Task Force's recommendations per se, the failure of the report to distinguish adequately among countries in the Balkan region results in less than substantive recommendations.

To varying degrees, Bulgaria, Macedonia, and Romania have undertaken the difficult process of democratic and economic reform, while others like Albania are just now emerging from years of chaos. Bulgaria especially has spent the last several years taking comprehensive and politically difficult measures in line with the recommendations of this report. Without acknowledging the current split status of the region, it is impossible to effectively prescribe long-term solutions. It should be also noted that a major problem for these countries has been the various economic embargos as well as the military campaign against Serbia.

In fact, the report recommends that countries willing to address their challenges should receive international support. Since several countries have already been addressing key issues, the question should be the level and type of international support commensurate with each country's progress to date.

Moreover, the report incorrectly insinuates to those outside the international investment world that investment does not come to the emerging markets or to countries without predictable, sophisticated legal systems. Of course, this is simply not the case. One has only to look from Siberia to Southeast Asia to Latin America to realize that foreign investment is dependent on myriad factors.

On the issue of corruption, the paper rebukes the European Union for its own corruption: "EU members that have not already passed the enabling legislation, or have not yet excluded bribes as a tax deduction, should act promptly to do so." Since the Task Force's main policy recommendation is that the EU is responsible for fixing the Balkans, this is an odd forum in which to lecture the Europeans on their internal matters.

Finally, the report neglects to recommend policy measures for the United States to follow. Since we will likely reenter the region militarily if there is another humanitarian disaster/security threat, the United States must embark on a meaningful course of action to further encourage the successful countries in the region to continue their reforms. One should look to the Marshall Plan for inspiration on how policymakers can look past the immediate and cultivate the permanent, despite large domestic political obstacles.

Hanya Marie Kim

TASK FORCE MEMBERS

REGINALD BARTHOLOMEW is Vice-Chairman of Merrill Lynch Europe, the Middle East, and Africa and Chairman of Merrill Lynch Italy. Ambassador Bartholomew is a former U.S. Foreign Service officer who served as Under Secretary of State and Ambassador to Lebanon, Spain, NATO, and Italy.

FRANCO BERNABÉ is Chairman of Andala UMTS SPA, an Italian independent telecommunications company, and former Chief Executive Office of Telecom Italia SPA. He is also serving as the Special Representative of the Italian government for the Reconstruction of the Balkan Region.

KEVIN CLOWE is Managing Director of AIG Capital Partners, a wholly owned subsidiary of the American International Group, Inc. He is actively involved in AIG's direct investment activities in Bulgaria and elsewhere in the emerging markets.

IVO H. DAALDER, a Senior Fellow at the Brookings Institution, was Director for European Affairs at the National Security Council from 1995 to 1996, where he was responsible for coordinating U.S. policy toward Bosnia. He is the author of *Getting to Dayton: The Making of America's Bosnia Policy* and the co-author of *Winning Ugly: NATO's War to Save Kosovo*, to be published by Brookings Institution Press in 2000.

FULVIO V. DOBRICH is President and Chief Executive Officer of DePfa USA Incorporated, a firm active in investment banking in emerging markets. As such he has been for over a decade actively managing investments in the countries of the Balkan Region. He is also Chairman of the U.S. Business Council for Southeastern Europe.

JAMES W. DYER is Clerk and Staff Director of the House Appropriations Committee. He previously worked on legislative and intergovernmental affairs for the U.S. House of Representatives, the U.S. Senate, the White House, State Department, and in the private sector.

LAWRENCE S. EAGLEBURGER is Senior International Affairs Adviser at Baker Donelson Bearman & Caldwell. Ambassador Eagleburger served as Secretary of State during 1992 and Ambassador to Yugoslavia from 1977 to 1981.

MICHAEL EMERSON is Senior Research Fellow at the Centre for European Policy Studies in Brussels and at the London School of Economics. Dr. Emerson formerly worked for the European Commission, including as Ambassador to Moscow from 1991 to 1996. He is the author of two recent articles, "The CEPS Plan for the Balkans" and "Redrawing the Map of Europe."

MICHAEL B.G. FROMAN is Director of Strategic Development at Citigroup. During this project, he was Senior Fellow at the Council on Foreign Relations and at the German Marshall Fund. Mr. Froman previously served as Deputy Assistant Secretary and Chief of Staff at the Treasury Department and on the staff of the National Economic Council and National Security Council at the White House.

MICHAEL D. GRANOFF is Chief Executive Officer of Pomona Capital, an international private equity investment company with over $580 million in capital. Mr. Granoff has previously served on the staff of the U.S. House of Representatives, as an Official Adviser to Annual Meetings of the World Bank/ International Monetary Fund, and as a member of the Presidential Transition Team at the Treasury Department. He was appointed by the President to the Board of the Albanian-American Enterprise Fund and is a director of the American Bank of Albania.

MICHAEL HALTZEL is Minority Staff Director of the Senate
Foreign Relations Subcommittee on European Affairs and
Senior Foreign Policy Adviser to Senator Joseph R. Biden
Jr. (D-Del.). Formerly Chief of the European Division of the
Library of Congress, Dr. Haltzel is lead Senate Democratic
staffer on Balkan issues and travels frequently to the region.

GLENN HUTCHINS is founder of Silver Lake Partners, the leading private equity firm investing in technology and related
growth businesses. From 1994 to 1999, he served as the
Chairman of the WNIS Enterprise Fund, which was established by Congress to assist in the development of the private
sector in Ukraine, Moldova, and Belarus. He also serves
as Vice Chairman of CARE, the international relief and
development organization.

ANDREW KENNINGHAM is Senior Economist with Merrill
Lynch specializing in central and eastern Europe, particularly
southeastern Europe. Mr. Kenningham lived and worked in
Bulgaria from 1991 to 1994.

HANYA MARIE KIM has spent over 11 years investing in the
United States, Asia, and Europe. She is the founding partner
of Intrepid International Partners, LP, an investment fund
for Bulgaria and the region. She has also worked on arms
control research for Paul H. Nitze and military strategy
issues with the Center for Naval Analyses.

SUSAN LEVINE is Managing Director of JER Partners, the real
estate investment arm of the J.E. Robert Companies. She
previously served at the Overseas Private Investment Corpo-
ration and the U.S. Treasury Department.

SCOTT LILLY is Minority Staff Director of the House Appropriations Committee, responsible for managing the minority
staff of the committee and recommending legislative strategies on spending to the committee Democrats and House
Democratic Leadership. Previously, he served as Clerk and

Staff Director to the House Appropriations Committee, Executive Director of the House Democratic Study Group, and Executive Director of the Joint Economic Committee.

DAVID LIPTON is Managing Director at Moore Capital Strategy Group. He previously served as Under Secretary for International Affairs at the U.S. Treasury Department, where he had extensive involvement in U.S. policymaking in the Balkan region.

WILLIAM LUERS is Chairman and President of the United Nations Association of the USA. Ambassador Luers was President of the Metropolitan Museum of Art from 1986 to 1999. Before that he served in the U.S. Foreign Service for 30 years, during which time he held many senior positions connected to central Europe and the former Soviet Union. Ambassador Luers's last assignment was as U.S. Ambassador to Czechoslovakia.

MARGARET F. MUDD is a Senior Adviser at the Financial Services Volunteer Corps in New York, a not-for-profit organization that helps countries develop the financial infrastructure necessary to support transparent, market-oriented economies. Ms. Mudd spent 18 years working in the international banking departments of two U.S. banks, a large part of which was devoted to financing transactions in eastern Europe and in the Balkans.

ALAN RAPPAPORT is Partner of The Beacon Group. During the past ten years while at CIBC Oppenheimer, Mr. Rappaport has sponsored numerous investment funds focused on investing in private and public companies in the emerging markets.

STEVEN RATTNER is Deputy Chairman of the investment banking firm, Lazard Frères & Co. LLC.

KLAUS REGLING is Managing Director of Moore Capital Strategy Group, London. Previously, he worked at the International Monetary Fund and at the German Ministry of Finance, including as Director General for European and International Financial Relations from 1995 to 1998.

MARIE ROBSON is a recently retired Vice President of Citibank, responsible for building the central and east European financial institutions business for the past 12 years. She is also Vice Chair of the U.S. Business Council for Southeastern Europe, a not-for-profit organization whose aim is to promote trade and investment in the region.

DAVID ROTHKOPF is Co-founder and Chairman/Chief Executive Officer of the Newmarket Company, a Washington, D.C.–based provider of international information and advisory services specializing in the world's emerging markets. He is also an Adjunct Professor of international affairs at Columbia University and Georgetown University. Previously, he served as Managing Director and Member of the Board of Kissinger Associates, Incorporated, and as Acting Under Secretary of Commerce for International Trade, among other senior positions at the Commerce Department.

PAUL M. SACKS is President of MNS, a consulting firm focusing on a series of high-level assignments in central Europe supporting privatization. Dr. Sacks has been a consultant for the U.S. Agency for International Development privatization program in Czechoslovakia and designed and established MNS's privatization advisory and capital markets projects in Albania, Romania, Estonia, and the Newly Independent States.

ERIC SHAW is Director and Head of Enron's Central European Business Activities. He has been active in central and eastern Europe for over five years and has successfully implemented a number of business initiatives in a wide range of southeast European countries.

LAURA SILBER, visiting Associate at the Remarque Institute at New York University, is co-author of the critically acclaimed *Yugoslavia: Death of a Nation.* She was based in the former Yugoslavia for a decade, first as a Fulbright scholar and then as a reporter for the *Financial Times.*

GEORGE SOROS is Chairman of Soros Fund Management LCC. He funds a network of foundations dedicated to building and maintaining the infrastructure and institutions of an open society.

ERNEST STERN is Managing Director at J.P. Morgan for senior relations with emerging market economies. He has more than 35 years experience in developing and transition economies. Mr. Stern served at the U.S. Agency for International Development, where his last position was Assistant Administrator, and then for 25 years at the World Bank, where he was Chief Operating Officer, Chief Financial Officer, and Senior Managing Director, with responsibilities including eastern and central Europe.

PAUL G. YOVOVICH is a private investor and a principal of Lake Capital Management. He is also a director of a number of public and private companies, primarily in the technology and business service sectors.

BOB ZANE is Senior Vice President, Manufacturing and Sourcing for Liz Claiborne Incorporated. Liz Claiborne produces more than 120,000,000 apparel and accessory units annually, in contractor-owned factories throughout the world.

TASK FORCE OBSERVERS

CARL BILDT is the U.N. Special Envoy for the Balkans responsible for advocacy on behalf of countries in the region affected by the Kosovo crisis, representing the United Nations in the work of the Stability Pact for Southeastern Europe. Mr. Bildt was the High Representative for Bosnia from 1995 to 1997 and the Prime Minister of Sweden from 1991 to 1994.

LOJOS BOKROS is Director of Financial Advisory Services in the Europe and Central Asia region of the World Bank. Mr. Bokros has been instrumental in designing and implementing financial and private sector reform in many transition economies, including Slovakia, Romania, Bulgaria, and Albania. Mr. Bokros was Finance Minister of Hungary from 1995 to 1996.

FRASER CAMERON is Head of the Political Section at the European Union Delegation in Washington, D.C. He was formerly Foreign Policy Adviser to Commissioner Hans van den Broek and has been closely involved in developing European Union policies toward the countries of southern Europe. A former academic and diplomat, he is the author of numerous articles and books on European foreign and security policy.

ROBERT CORKER is Adviser in the European I Department of the International Monetary Fund. Mr. Corker currently leads missions to Albania and coordinates IMF work on Kosovo and southeast Europe. He formerly headed IMF missions to the Former Yugoslav Republic of Macedonia.

DAVID DE PURY is Chairman of de Pury Pictet Turrettini & Co. Ltd, a Swiss-based investment firm. He is a former Co-chairman of the ABB Group and a former Swiss Trade Ambassador. David de Pury is Publisher and Chairman of the Swiss daily newspaper, *Le Temps*, and serves on the boards of several multinational corporations and nonprofit organizations.

PIERRE KELLER retired after 34 years at Lombard, Odier & Cie. Most recently, he was Chairman of Lombard, Odier International Portfolio Management Limited and Senior Partner of the bank from 1990 to 1994. Previously, he served in the Swiss Diplomatic Service assigned to the Swiss Observer's Office to the United Nations, the Federal Political Department in Berne, and the Swiss delegation to the European Free Trade Association in Geneva.

CHARLES A. KUPCHAN is Senior Fellow at the Council on Foreign Relations and Associate Professor of international relations in the School of Foreign Service and Government Department at Georgetown University. Dr. Kupchan was Director for European Affairs on the National Security Council during the first Clinton administration and has worked in the U.S. Department of State on the Policy Planning Staff. Prior to government service, he was an Assistant Professor of politics at Princeton University.

APPENDIXES

HOW THE INTERNATIONAL COMMUNITY IS ORGANIZED TO PROMOTE STABILITY AND RECOVERY IN KOSOVO AND SOUTHEAST EUROPE

Stability Pact

Signed on July 30, 1999, the Stability Pact is an initiative of 27 democracies that seeks to strengthen the efforts of southeast European countries to foster peace, democracy, respect for human rights, and economic prosperity. Its goal is to stabilize, transform, and eventually integrate the entire region into the European and transatlantic mainstream.

Stability Pact participants include all member states of the European Union (EU), the European Commission, the United States, Russia, Canada, Japan, Hungary, Ukraine, Moldova, Turkey, Albania, Bosnia-Herzegovina, Bulgaria, Croatia, Hungary, Romania, the Former Yugoslav Republic of Macedonia, and Slovenia.

The position of special coordinator and several regional forums were established to help countries of the region and donors work together more closely in advancing these goals.

The special coordinator of the Stability Pact, who is appointed by the EU, has responsibility for promoting achievement of the Stability Pact's objectives and chairing the Southeast Europe Regional Table. Bodo Hombach, former chief of staff to German Chancellor Schroeder, was selected for this position. Donald Kursch, a senior State Department foreign service officer, serves as his principal deputy. The special coordinator has a staff of 15 to 20, mainly seconded officials from European Union members and the United States.

The Southeast Europe Regional Table acts as the steering body for the Stability Pact process and clearinghouse for questions of principle relating to its implementation. The regional table provides policy guidance to the three working tables.

The Working Table on Democracy and Human Rights focuses on democratic reform, human rights, free media, civil society building, the rule of law, good governance, border issues, and the return and protection of refugees.

The Working Table on Economic Reconstruction, Development, and Cooperation addresses a broad range of economic issues, including reconstruction, economic reform, regional cooperation, the promotion of free trade, regional transportation, energy, private sector development, and environmental issues.

The Working Table on Security has responsibility for three main areas: measures to combat organized crime, corruption, terrorism, and other illegal activities; arms control and confidence-building measures; and cooperation on defense and military issues aimed at enhancing stability in the region and preventing military conflict.

High-Level Steering Group for Southeast Europe
Heads of state at the EU Summit in Cologne established the High-Level Steering Group (HLSG) to provide strategic direction and donor coordination for the economic reconstruction, stabilization, reform, and development of the southeast Europe region. The HLSG is co-chaired by European Commissioner for Economic and Monetary Affairs Pedro Solbes Mira and World Bank President James Wolfensohn.

Members include the finance ministers of the United States, Canada, France, Germany, Italy, Japan, Russia, the United Kingdom, and Finland (representing the presidency of the European Union), the managing director of the International Monetary Fund (IMF), the president of the European Bank for Reconstruction and Development (EBRD), the president of the European Investment Bank, the special coordinator of the Stability Pact for Southeastern Europe, and the deputy secretary general of the United Nations. A representative of the U.N. Mission in Kosovo (UNMIK) and senior development ministers of donor countries also attend HLSG meetings. The work of the HLSG is supported by a Working-Level Steering Group (WLSG) composed of senior officials from member governments and international organizations.

The HLSG met on July 23, 1999, and September 24, 1999, to review the economic consequences of the hostilities in Kosovo and begin planning new initiatives to promote the economic recovery and revitalization of southeast Europe. A third meeting is planned for early 2000. In carrying out its work, the HLSG is coordinating closely with the Stability Pact and its Working Tables, in particular the Table on Economic Reconstruction, Development, and Cooperation.

Joint World Bank/European Commission Office on Southeast Europe
The World Bank and European Commission have established a joint office in Brussels to organize donor coordination meetings and prepare analytical work on the economic needs of Kosovo and the southeast European region. The meetings are chaired by Fabrizio Barbaso, the European Commission's director for the western Balkans, and Christiaan Poortman, the World Bank country director and regional coordinator for southeast Europe.

In July-December 1999, the joint office organized two international donors conferences on Kosovo. At the first conference held on July 28, 1999, donors made preliminary pledges of $2.1 billion to assist in Kosovo's recovery. On November 16, 1999, a second conference was held to review assistance needs over the next year. At that conference, which senior officials from 47 donor countries and 34 international organizations attended, pledges for $1 billion were made to support reconstruction through 2000. To assist donors in developing assistance initiatives, the World Bank and European Commission have prepared detailed analyses on the economic problems facing Kosovo, the costs of addressing them, and possible strategies for implementing a plan of action.

A third donors conference that will focus on the infrastructure needs of the entire southeast Europe region is planned for February/March 2000. The conference will use procedures agreed at the Istanbul Summit in November 1999 to begin vetting and refining regional projects and to explore possible donor financing.

Office of the High Representative for Bosnia Peace Implementation

Wolfgang Petritsch, former Austrian ambassador to Yugoslavia and EU chief negotiator at the Kosovo peace talks, was appointed the High Representative for Bosnia-Herzegovina in August 1999. He and his international staff of 260, many seconded diplomats from the United States and European countries, are responsible for civilian implementation of the Bosnian Peace Agreement (i.e., the Dayton Accords).

U.N. Mission in Kosovo

The United Nations established the U.N. Mission in Kosovo (UNMIK) to serve as the international authority for Kosovo and to carry out the mandate of U.N. Security Council Resolution 1244. The UNMIK is headed by Special Representative of the Secretary General (SRSG) Bernard Kouchner (France). His principal deputy is Jock Covey (United States). The deputy special representatives for the four functions of the UNMIK are:

- Interim Civil Administration: Dominique Vian (United Nations)

- Humanitarian Affairs: Dennis McNamara (UNHCR)

- Institution-Building: Daan Everts (OSCE)

- Reconstruction: Joly Dixon (European Commission)

European Union
Responsibility for developing and implementing EU policy on the Balkans is divided between the European Commission and the Council of Ministers, the EU's intergovernmental policy-making forum. As the current commission president and a former Italian prime minister, Romano Prodi has played an active role in developing policy proposals on the Balkans and presenting the EU's positions in the public arena. Within the commission itself, implementation of EU policy cuts across several functional areas, including external economic affairs, external political affairs, enlargement, economic and financial affairs, and development assistance. Key roles in managing southeast Europe policy are played by Commissioner for External Affairs Chris Patten, Commissioner for Economic and Monetary Affairs Pedro Solbes Mira, and Commissioner for Enlargement Gunter Verheugen.

Responsibility for day-to-day commission coordination falls to the Western Balkans Office in the Directorate General for External Relations. Assistance activities are carried out under the PHARE program, which administers EU aid to all former communist countries in central and southeast Europe. The Commission, however, has established a special task force on Kosovo to assess reconstruction needs and develop project proposals. In early 2000, the Commission plans to replace the task force with the new European Agency for Reconstruction, which will have responsibility for disbursing reconstruction funds in Kosovo.

From July through December 1999, Finland has represented European Union members on foreign policy and security issues in its capacity as the EU's rotating presidency country. EU foreign policy positions are established by the EU Council of Ministers, which, in turn, provides direction to the European Commission. As the presidency spokesman for the council, the Finnish foreign minister has played an active role in policy discussions on the Balkans. The EU presidency rotates to Portugal during January-June 2000 and then France during July-December 2000.

The newly established position of EU High Representative for Common Foreign and Security Policy, now held by Javier Solana, assists the Council of Ministers in formulating policy and conducting dialogue with foreign governments, including on issues relating to southeast Europe. In his capacity as special coordinator for the Stability Pact, Bodo Hombach serves as a special representative of the Council of Ministers.

United States

Several U.S. agencies are engaged in developing and implementing U.S. policy on the Balkans and carrying out Stability Pact–related activities. The National Security Council, most notably the Office for Southeast European affairs, and the National Economic Council provide senior-level political guidance. Multiple offices of the State Department are involved in coordinating and implementing U.S. policy initiatives, including the office of the under secretary for economic affairs, the European affairs bureau, the policy planning office, and the economic affairs bureau.

The State Department is using a number of special coordinators and representatives to assist in policy implementation. They include the coordinator for Stability Pact Implementation and Southeast Europe Initiatives (Dan Hamilton), the coordinator for Eastern European Assistance (Larry Napper), the coordinator for Southeast Europe Cooperative Initiatives (Richard Schifter), the special adviser for Kosovo and Dayton Implementation (James Dobbins), and the special representative for Southeast Europe Initiatives (Richard Sklar, resident in Rome).

In addition to the State Department, several other U.S. agencies are actively involved in supporting U.S. policy goals in southeast Europe and implementing Stability Pact initiatives. The Treasury Department develops U.S. financial policies toward the Balkans and coordinates with international financial institutions, notably the World Bank, IMF, and EBRD. The U.S. Agency for International Development (USAID) develops and carries out most U.S. assistance programs in Balkan countries. Finally, the Commerce Department facilitates business input into the economic table and provides policy advice on improving conditions for foreign investment and private sector development.

SUMMARY OF INTERNATIONAL ASSISTANCE INITIATIVES FOR KOSOVO AND SOUTHEAST EUROPE

European Union

For the period 2000–06, the European Union (EU) is planning to finance assistance programs totaling 5 billion euros ($5.2 billion) for Albania, Bosnia, Croatia, Macedonia, and Yugoslavia/Kosovo. An additional 6.2 billion euros ($6.4 billion) in pre-accession assistance to Bulgaria and Romania is being proposed for the same period. The EU has committed 500 million euros ($527 million) to assist Kosovo with reconstruction from November 1999 through December 2000.[1] In 1991–99, EU programs, including the European Investment Bank, provided more than 8.9 billion euros ($9.2 billion) to southeast Europe in a variety of assistance programs (humanitarian aid, reconstruction assistance, infrastructure loans, and economic and financial support). Separately EU members have extended aid to the region totaling 6.4 billion euros ($6.6 billion).

United States

In fiscal year 2000, the United States will devote $523 million to southeast Europe, out of its total $533 million in economic assistance funding for European transitioning economies. (This does not include humanitarian and other types of U.S. assistance.) Kosovo will receive $142 million of that amount. The total U.S. aid commitment to Kosovo from November 1999 through December 2000 is $157 million. In fiscal years 1991–99, the United States provided economic assistance totaling $2.0

---

[1] In the announcement of its aid pledge of 500 million euros, the EU converted its dollar equivalent at the rate prevailing on November 17, 1999, of euro 1.00 = $1.05. The more current rate of euro 1.00 = $1.03, however, was used in this report to convert all other euro figures.

billion to Albania, Bosnia, Bulgaria, Croatia, Macedonia, and Romania.[2]

World Bank

Balkan Countries. In 1998–99, the World Bank launched new projects in the region amounting to more than $1.6 billion. Since 1991, the Bank has undertaken 139 projects or major operations involving commitments of $6.6 billion in Albania, Bosnia, Bulgaria, Croatia, Macedonia, and Romania. In addition to large infrastructure projects, the World Bank is financing activities in the fields of health, community development, agricultural and forestry development, enterprise privatization, land registration, pensions, and small and medium-size enterprise (SME) development.

Kosovo. The World Bank expects to fund assistance programs amounting to $50 million to $60 million through its Special Trust Fund. The first tranche of $25 million will be used to provide budget support to cover the costs of health and education activities; finance inputs for farmers to begin the 2000 spring planting; and start a credit line for small and medium-size private businesses. A second tranche will be made available in the next fiscal year. The World Bank is also providing technical assistance to help start up the Kosovo Community Development Fund, which is being financed by the Soros Foundation. The fund will provide rapid targeted support to communities and local governments to help rebuild infrastructure and support essential services.

International Monetary Fund

Balkan Countries. In 1999, the International Monetary Fund (IMF) approved new drawings for Albania, Bosnia, Bulgaria, Macedonia, and Romania totaling approximately $691 million. From January 1, 1991, through November 30, 1999, the IMF extended $4.7 billion in loans to the above five countries and

---

[2]Includes economic assistance granted under the SEED Act but not humanitarian assistance and aid from other programs.

Croatia. The balance of loans outstanding as of November 30, 1999, was $2.2 billion. Loans were provided through the General Resources Account, the Structural Adjustment Facility, the Enhanced Structural Adjustment Facility, and the IMF Trust Fund.

Kosovo. The IMF is providing technical assistance to Kosovo on setting up a payments system and establishing a fiscal structure. On the payments system, the initial focus has been on facilitating local payments and transfers by the transitional authorities. IMF experts are also working with World Bank officials to draw up regulations for licensing and supervising banks under a new banking law. On the fiscal system, the priority has been to begin mobilizing tax revenues and organize budgetary and treasury systems. IMF experts are helping the U.N. Mission in Kosovo (UNMIK) to establish a central fiscal agency for Kosovo and project revenues and expenditures through 2000.

European Bank for Reconstruction and Development

The European Bank for Reconstruction Development (EBRD) has established a Southeast European Regional Action Plan (SERAP) to promote private sector development in the region. SERAP has three specific goals:

- Support private sector investment, including large corporations, SMEs, and microenterprises;

- Develop commercial approaches to financing infrastructure, including telecommunications, airports, and municipal projects; and

- Improve the institutional capacity of the financial sector, in particular institutions to support SMEs and microlending.

In addition to the SERAP, the EBRD has developed a Kosovo Action Plan (KAP) to assess investment opportunities there, identify potential partners, and establish a legal basis for activities. An EBRD office will be opening in Pristina to assist in implementing the KAP.

In light of the high-risk environment in the region, the EBRD has asked members to contribute to a Balkan Region Special Fund that would provide grant funds to help execute SERAP and KAP projects. Contributions to the fund are expected to exceed $100 million.

As of mid-June, the EBRD had committed $2.5 billion to 107 projects and mobilized a total of $9.3 billion of investment in southeast European countries. Projects include:

Albania:	microlending;
Bosnia:	trade facilitation;
Bulgaria:	financing for SME lending and agricultural trade, restructuring a wholesale market, trade facilitation, and power transmission;
Croatia:	upgrading tourist facilities in Dubrovnik;
Macedonia:	trade facilitation, SME lending program, and pharmaceuticals production;
Romania:	trade financing through four local banks.

Table 1. **International Aid Commitments to Kosovo at Donors Meeting, July 28, 1999**
(millions of dollars)

Donor	Humani-tarian	Civil Administration or U.N. Trust Fund	Other Urgent Programs	Total
EU	392	0	142	534
EU Members	484	23	98	605
United States	279	4	274	557
Japan	60	0	100	160
Other Bilateral Donors[a]	164	3	49	215
World Bank			60	60
Other Multilateral Donors[b]	32	5		37
Total[c]	1,411	34	722	2,168

Source: Press release of European Commission Delegation to the United States, August 12, 1999; European Commission Delegation mission to the United States website (www.eurunion.org).

[a] Includes Australia, Norway, Slovakia, Switzerland, and Turkey.
[b] Includes UNDP, UNICEF, and CE Social Development Fund.
[c] Some totals may not add due to rounding.

Table 2. International Aid Commitments to Kosovo for Recovery Needs, November 1999–December 2000[a]
(millions of dollars)

Donor	Amount
EU Members	236
EU Programs	527[b]
United States	157[c]
Others	136
Total	1,056

Source: World Bank/European Commission webpage on Economic Reconstruction and Development in Southeast Europe (www.seerecon.org).

[a]Commitments made at the donor coordination meeting held in Brussels on November 17, 1999.

[b]The EU pledged 500 million euros. Dollar amount is based on exchange rate on date of meeting.

[c]U.S. law limits the U.S. contribution in any fiscal year to no more than 15 percent of the total international aid commitments. The U.S. commitment for fiscal year 2000 (October 1, 1999 through September 30, 2000) is $142 million.

Table 3. Breakdown of U.S. Aid Commitments to Kosovo, November 1999–December 2000[a]
(millions of dollars)

Program	Amount
Economic Reforms	6
Agriculture	4
Human Services Infrastructure	10
Criminal Courts	2
Administration of Justice	5
International Police	48
Police Training	20
KPC	15
Demining	4
UNMIK Budget	5
Media	4
OSCE/Elections	25
Civic Education	9
Total	157

Source: U.S. State Department and World Bank/European Commission web-page on Economic Reconstruction and Development in Southeast Europe (www.seerecon.org).

[a]Commitments made at the aid coordination conference in Brussels on November 17, 1999.

Table 4. EU Assistance to Balkan Countries, 1991–99[a]
(millions of dollars)[b]

Country	EU	European Investment Bank	EU Members	Total
Albania	842	47	733	1,622
Bosnia	2,124	0	523	2,647
Bulgaria	1,525	778	774	3,077
Croatia	365	0	1,201	1,566
Macedonia	416	62	183	661
Romania	1,867	1,169	3,161	6,197
Total	7,139	2,056	6,575[c]	15,770

Source: EU press release dated November 19, 1999.

[a]Includes assistance for economic programs, democracy, institution-building, humanitarian aid, balance-of-payments support, and infrastructure.
[b]Converted from euro figures at euro 1.00 = $1.03.
[c]Total aid for period 1991–97.

Table 5. U.S. Assistance Funding for Balkan Countries: Economic Restructuring, Institution-Building, and Social Development Programs, Fiscal Year 1991–99[a]
(millions of dollars)

Country	Amount
Albania	217
Bosnia	958
Bulgaria	296
Croatia	99
Macedonia	109
Romania	278
Total	1,957

Source: U.S. State Department.

[a]U.S. assistance provided through SEED Act funding. Does not include substantial humanitarian assistance provided under other programs.

Table 6. EBRD Projects in Balkan Countries, June 30, 1999

Country	Number of Projects Signed	Commitments (millions of dollars)[a]
Albania	8	73
Bosnia	8	76
Bulgaria	20	302
Croatia	21	533
FYR Macedonia	8	150
Romania	58	1,414
Total Projects in region[b]	107	2,548

Source: See the EBRD website (www.ebrd.org).

[a] Converted from euro figures at euro 1 = $1.03.
[b] According to EBRD data, total projects for the region are not cumulative.

Table 7. World Bank Assistance Commitments to Balkan Countries, 1991–99 (millions of dollars)

Country	Amount	Projects/Operations
Albania	482	33
Bosnia	696	29
Bulgaria	1,134	18
Croatia	762	15
Macedonia	500	17
Romania	3,000	27
Total	6,574	139

Source: World Bank website (www.worldbank.org). Data as of November 30, 1999.

Table 8. IMF Activities in Balkan Countries: Disbursements and Repayments, January 1, 1991–November 30, 1999; Current Balances and New Commitments in 1999
(millions of dollars)[a]

Country	Disburse-ments	Repay-ments	Current Balance	New Commitments in 1999
Albania	102	22	80	30[b]
Bosnia	142	44	99	23[c]
Bulgaria	2,156	816	1,341	72[d]
Croatia	297	149	148	0
Macedonia	132	29	103	19[e]
Romania	1,864	1,400	464	547[f]
Total	4,693	2,460	2,235	691

Source: IMF press releases and website (www.imf.org). Some totals do not add because of rounding.

[a]SDR figures converted at SDR 1.00 = $1.37, average rate for November 1999.
[b]2nd installment under ESAF approved June 14, 1999.
[c]Augmentation of earlier Standby Credit.
[d]Partial disbursement of previous Standby Credit approved September 15, 1999.
[e]Drawing under Compensatory and Contingency Financing Facility approved August 5, 1999.
[f]Eight-month Standby Credit of which first installment is $73 million.

OTHER REPORTS OF INDEPENDENT TASK FORCES
SPONSORED BY THE COUNCIL ON FOREIGN RELATIONS

*†*Nonlethal Technologies: Progress and Prospects* (1999)
Richard L. Garwin, Chairman; W. Montague Winfield, Project Director

*†*U.S. Policy Toward North Korea: Next Steps* (1999)
Morton I. Abramowitz and James T. Laney, Co-Chairs; Michael J. Green, Project Director

†*Safegarding Prosperity in a Global System: The Future International Financial Architecture* (1999)
Carla A. Hills and Peter G. Peterson, Co-Chairs; Morris Goldstein, Project Director

*†*Strengthening Palestinian Public Institutions* (1999)
Michael Rocard, Chair; Henry Siegman, Project Director

*†*U.S. Policy Toward Northeastern Europe* (1999)
Zbigniew Brzezinski, Chairman; F. Stephen Larrabee, Project Director

*†*The Future of Transatlantic Relations* (1999)
Robert D. Blackwill, Chair and Project Director

*†*U.S.-Cuban Relations in the 21st Century* (1999)
Bernard W. Aronson and William D. Rogers, Co-Chairs; Walter Russell Mead, Project Director

*†*After the Tests: U.S. Policy Toward India and Pakistan* (1998)
Richard N. Haass and Morton H. Halperin, Co-Chairs; Cosponsored by the Brookings Institution

*†*Managing Change on the Korean Peninsula* (1998)
Morton I. Abramowitz and James T. Laney, Co-Chairs; Michael J. Green, Project Director

*†*Promoting U.S. Economic Relations with Africa* (1998)
Peggy Dulany and Frank Savage, Co-Chairs; Salih Booker, Project Director

†*U.S. Middle East Policy and the Peace Process* (1997)
Henry Siegman, Project Director

†*Russia, Its Neighbors, and an Enlarging NATO* (1997)
Richard G. Lugar, Chair; Victoria Nuland, Project Director

*†*Differentiated Containment: U.S. Policy Toward Iran and Iraq* (1997)
Zbigniew Brzezinski and Brent Scowcroft, Co-Chairs; Richard Murphy, Project Director

Rethinking International Drug Control: New Directors for U.S. Policy (1997)
Mathea Falco, Chair and Project Director

*†*Financing America's Leadership: Protecting American Interests and Promoting American Values* (1997)
Mickey Edwards and Stephen J. Solarz, Co-Chairs; Morton H. Halperin, Lawrence J. Korb, and Richard M. Moose, Project Directors

†*A New U.S. Policy Toward India and Pakistan* (1997)
Richard N. Haass, Chair; Gideon Rose, Project Director

†*Arms Control and the U.S.-Russian Relationship: Problems, Prospects, and Prescriptions* (1996)
Robert D. Blackwill, Chair and Author; Keith W. Dayton, Project Director; Cosponsored with the Nixon Center

†*American National Interests and the United Nations* (1996)
George Soros, Chair

---

*Available from Brookings Institution Press. To order, call 1-800-275-1447.
†Available on the Council on Foreign Relations website at www.cfr.org.